ANCHOR
BOOKS

*JOYFUL THOUGHTS
OF CHRISTMAS*

Edited by

Bobby Tobolik

First published in Great Britain in 2005 by
ANCHOR BOOKS
Remus House,
Coltsfoot Drive,
Peterborough, PE2 9JX
Telephone (01733) 898102

Copyright Contributors 2005

SB ISBN 1 84418 401 3

FOREWORD

Anchor Books is a small press, established in 1992, with the aim of promoting readable poetry to as wide an audience as possible.

We hope to establish an outlet for writers of poetry who may have struggled to see their work in print.

The poems presented here have been selected from many entries, and as always editing proved to be a difficult task.

I trust this selection will delight and please the authors and all those who enjoy reading poetry.

Bobby Tobolik
Editor

CONTENTS

SANTA'S ROBINS

Have you ever stopped to wonder how every Christmas Eve
Old Santa knows just where to go and knows just what to leave?
He knows each little girl and boy and whether they've been good,
He knows which child desires which toy; and gives it, if he should.

The answer to this mystery was told me by a bird -
A cheeky little redbreast - it's true, I give my word!
Yes, Santa's little robins with their bright and beady eyes
Can see straight into children's hearts; can tell the truth from lies.

Next time you see a redbreast come hopping through the snow
You can bet it's telling Santa just what he needs to know.
So be kind to Santa's robins and give them lots to eat:
That way next year at Christmas you will get an extra treat!

Anne Wild

POLAR BEER

A miserable, mournful and bored polar bear
sat staring at icebergs and sniffing the air,
When along came the thump of galloping hooves
and the jingle of sleigh bells in jovial tunes -
'Whoa! What have we here?' said a merry, white beard
in a hooded red suit, holding reins as they reared.
'That's a miserable bear who's all on his own.
We'll soon change all that!' Old Santa declared
and emptied a sack over polar bear's home.
'It's the time of goodwill and the season of cheer.
Let the penguins who wait on us, pour out the beer.'
So each had a mugful - including the deer.

Rosemary Keith

HAPPY MORN

I hung a sock above my head
On the post of my oak bedstead,
I know Santa is very quiet,
He won't wake me. He has no desire.
He tiptoes all around,
Never makes the slightest sound
While putting down gifts he brings,
Santa really is a Fairy King.
I woke next morn
And looked around,
Toys lay neatly on the ground.
Oh what joy he brought to me,
Just look around and you will see.
Thanks Santa. God bless you!

Peggy Johnson

DEAR SANTA

Dear Santa
On Christmas Day I finished up at A and E,
I suppose it was very clumsy of me.
As I flourished my brand new Christmas knives,
Slicing the turkey, my hand gave a dive,
Forgetting their steely-honed edge
I sliced my fingers and bled all over the veg.
Christmas in the Emergency Room as my
Stitched fingers freeze.
So Santa next year, something safe for me, please!

Mary Spence

UNTITLED

I think this might be the last year
for a visit from Santa
As but for help from reindeers
Dasher and Dancer
In the top of the chimney he would
have been stuck -
So for 2005's diet, I wish him luck!

Doreen Yewdall

RUDOLPH'S RESTITUTION

I'm having a rest this Christmas,
My duties are pie in the sky.
It's time for a stand-off
Let Santa get Randolph
I'll stay here till New Year, that's why!

Patricia Jeanne Hale

A FERVENT WISH

Santa, in your magic castle
Way up in the Northern Star
Will you hear my silent wishes
Sent you from a place afar?

Santa, in your icy homeland
Frozen as in time and space
Will you next year, bring the present
Dearest to my heart, your grace?

Opal Innsbruk

FATHER CHRISTMAS

The drink and food on hearth is laid,
The special treat for reindeer made;
The children climb the stairs to bed,
With thoughts of presents in their heads.

The night is long and sky is clear,
The time for Santa now is near;
The sleigh bells ring with heavenly joy,
There's gifts for girls and for boys.

The drink and food all fade away,
As dawn doth break on Christmas Day;
The children's eyes just glow with joy,
As they all glimpse their brand new toys.

To Santa, thanks and prayers are made,
As sounds of tinkling bells just fade;
That magic and joy that Santa brings,
Long may the sleigh bells loudly ring.

John Paulley

WISHES FOR CHRISTMAS

If I had a teddy all of my own
I would not swap it for a garden gnome
I would keep it and cuddle it in my bed
And use his fat tummy for my head

I've wished for a teddy for Christmas time
And if I get one I know he is mine
I can't wait for Christmas to look under the tree
To see if Santa will be good to me

Oh look under the tree, there are presents for me
I wonder what's in them, please let me see
I must have been good, there is a bear
Oh thank you Santa, you've given me a pair!

P R Ward

MY SON'S FRIEND, SANTA

I've often been to Scotland for pleasure and for work
And I've drunk their National Nectar with director and with clerk.
My grandad introduced it and its pleasure to me
Each time we could afford it, we'd have one (or maybe three)
As a child I loved Santa Claus, as I still do today
And 'Pa' told me he loved a glass of Scotch to help him on his way.
So I'd place a glass in the fireplace, near the Christmas tree,
And on Christmas morning, an empty glass and presents just for me.
So I grew to love Scotch whisky and to share it with best friends
Whether straight, malt or blended, its pleasure never ends.
And now my five year old son knows my pleasure
Of pouring the whisky down my throat, a moment to treasure.
When he grows up, he says, like me, it'll be the drink of friends
He knows my passion for it, the one that never ends.
So tonight on Christmas Eve, by the tree he'll leave a dram
Of my finest malt, for that white bearded, wonderful man,
And that malt whisky is not wasted as Santa will drink it to its end,
It will have been enjoyed by one of my son's greatest friends.

Mike Jackson

DEAR SANTA *(OR WHERE'S MY PRESENT?)*

Dear Santa
Have you missed me Santa
As much as I've missed you?
Have you read my Christmas List
And wrapped my presents too?
Have you loaded up your sleigh
And polished up your lamp?
Could you read the map I drew?
(It may have got quite damp!)
I posted it at Hallowe'en
I couldn't bear to wait
The days and weeks that yawn between
Our special Christmas date.
I promised to be good *all* year!
And kind and right and fair
And I've been so, Mummy says
I've even learned to share!
Santa, are you proud of me?
Has my sweetness made you jolly?
If so, dear Santa, then please, please, please
Please may I have a dolly?

Lynda Kathryn Robinson

SANTA

Oh Santa dear - I have to warn
The chimney's rather narrow
And not designed for reindeer,
But more likely for a sparrow.

And don't come on a Wednesday
That day the 'sweep' is due
He may make some improvement
With his brushes to the flue

But then again the pictures of you
Show you rather stout
If you succeed in getting in
You still have to come out

So if it helps I'll leave the
Back door open and unlocked
And leave a heavy overcoat
In case you get de-frocked!

Leonard T Coleman

LITTLE REINDEER

Does little reindeer wait in vain?
Will Santa need his help again?

The snow is falling gently now,
Night temperature is dropping low,
His breath plumes upward in frosty air,
The waiting is so hard to bear.

But just when hope seems all but gone,
There's a shooting star to wish upon,
And ere that wish was whispered low,
Santa came trudging through the snow.

'Come quickly now,' the old man said,
'All the children are going to bed,
I need you now, help pull my sleigh,
Through all the countries near and away!'

The 'Aurora B' lights up the sky,
They hop on-board her straight away,
That magic bridge, red, gold and green,
Most beautiful thing ever to be seen.

So little reindeer's wish came true,
To bring the gifts to me and you.

Dorothy Ellis

SANTA

What do you do
When Christmas is through?
Stable the reindeer
Make a fresh brew?
Fold up the sacks,
Now the presents have gone.
File all the letters,
Now the job's done.
Hope all the children
Have what they hold dear.
Put up your feet
And wait for next year!

A Homewood

UNTITLED

Dear Santa,
I must write to you, so here goes . . .
My boy is only three but the toys
he wants, he knows.
I know my son can't write or read.
So I've been told to write down what he needs,
because he's watching me do it
to keep me right and in the Christmas spirit.
First there's a bike, a blue one would be nice,
and I know that he'll get it, because it's the right price.
Then there's a Power Ranger,
where's Action Man gone?
Who's this stranger?
Sweets and a jumper, no problem at all.
A Tweenies game, a what?
And a new football!
I have no idea who Tweenies are,
but if they're out there, he can rely on his Da!
Now Santa, you're great because
my son knows that you'll bring his presents
even if it snows.
I don't mind pretending to be you,
because Christmas is magic and for my boy, it's true.

Val Ramsey

A POEM FOR SANTA

Santa and his reindeers are on their way
With it being Christmas Day
Sleigh bells ring
As the children sing
Thank you for everything I wished for
Including the snow that is falling
While angels are calling
Now that Christmas is here
Along with the New Year.

Coleen Bradshaw

CHIRON
(The Mini Planet)

In 1977, on a day in that November,
Charles Kowal, an astronomer, did something we'll remember.
He had been taking photographs of bits of sky, in turn,
When all at once, between the paths of Uranus and Saturn,
On looking at a photograph he'd taken earlier on,
He saw a smudge, ferreted round and named the thing Chiron.
He thought it was a planet but it was so very small,
His colleagues thought that it must be an asteroid, withal.

Jillian Mounter

UNTITLED

Dear Santa
To us Irish kids you were known as Santy Claus
(Without the 'e'),
From a foreign country.
Never getting stuck
Nor giving a bother
For the coal dust or muck.
But now that chimneys are no more,
Surely your mission is finally o'er . . .

Over here, they call you Santa
(Even tho' St Nicholas does actually
Rhyme with Xmas).
So it's incumbent upon me
To inform you, Santy,
Of your redundancy -
The kids have seen thro' you.
No longer do they want ya'
Dear Santa.
Love, D.

Donagh Sanfey

A WING AND A PRAYER

Sleep child, sleep,
Santa's on his way.
Bringing gifts for
All of us, on this
Special day.
May your dreams become
Reality when you awaken
On Christmas Day, and find
What Santa's left for you
Before he went away.

Arnold Monk

SANTA

My real name's Saint Nicholas
From Myra in the east
In bishop's clothes
I gave away
Gold, secretly at least.

They heard of me in
Holland then
And called me Santa Claus,
Gave secret gifts to boys and girls
Who crossed to US shores.

Here then I saw a thousand men
All dressed in white and red
To lead the Christmas goings on
And gave good gifts instead.
Those Father Christmases soon felt
That they should follow me
And use my name but not my clothes,
Yes, they should Santa be.

So now when Father Christmas comes,
Giving gifts to girls and boys,
I am remembered by my name -
My name of Santa Claus.

Owen Edwards

DEAR SANTA

I've sent my letter early, to give you extra time,
To put a gift together for the people in my rhyme.
There are people all around this world, whose hearts are full of pain,
They come from every walk of life, some searching around in vain.
For Santa, in a sunny land, an earthquake took its toll
For far away beneath the sea, the earth was no more whole.
It made a hole in people's hearts that nobody can fix,
But in your bag of goodies, you may find lots of tricks.
Please ask the fairy on the tree to wave her magic wand,
Deliver happy memories, in person, by your hand.
For Santa if we all could send a little love today,
To all those hurting people who live so far away,
A kiss to make a sad face smile, a hug to make it better,
All wrapped inside my note for you . . .
Please Santa . . . read my letter.

Wendy Ann Evans

TO SANTA WITH THANKS

Thank you Santa for your suit of red,
For your snowy white beard,
For getting the children early to bed,
Thank you Santa for the excitement you bring,
The joy of your laugh,
For my diamond ring,
Thank you Santa for being fat,
I like to think,
I don't look like that,
Thank you Santa for being you,
No one else could do what you do,
Thank You Santa.

Jayne Harrison

SANTA

On a snowy, still winter's night
Santa came to town
Little children fast asleep
Tucked beneath the eiderdown
The reindeer's bells tinkled merrily
Upon the snow-topped roofs
And Santa with his sack of toys
For all the girls and boys
He stealthily slid down the chimney
Leaving presents beneath the tree
While Prancer, Dancer, Vixen and Rudolf
Waited patiently
His reindeer munched on lots of treats
Also Santa too
To keep their strength up for the night
And through the sky they flew
So if you see Santa Claus
On a very still Christmas night
Close your eyes and go to sleep
Sweet dreams until daylight.

Margery Rayson

UNTITLED

Dear Santa I wish nothing for me
But what I would wish for, is nations to be free
To dance, sing, laugh, to be fed and warm
Vote for whom they want, and come to no harm
Women and children seem to suffer the worst
In all forms of abuse, also hunger and thirst
So Santa, I'm asking for the so-called goodwill
For everyone in every land to be at peace and still.

Robert Henry

SANTA SAYS

Did you know your toys
Come to life at night?
Don't look so surprised,
They really do!
The teddies with their eyes so wide,
The dolls, the duck and the kangaroo.
They skip and jump and dance around,
Wishing you would wake.
Dance with them, hold their paws,
It would make the world just great.

Susan Haldenby

SANTA'S ON MY ROOF

I hear Santa on my roof.
Listen, you'll hear the jingles of his sleigh.
I wished for a great big Christmas pud
So we could share it on Christmas Day.
I only wish for simple things
Because I know he has a busy time
So I hope he enjoys his mince pie
And a glass of wine.

Carole Morris

UNTITLED

When I am asked what I want for Christmas,
people expect me to say, 'World peace.'
I must look sanctimonious in the extreme.
Of course it would be wonderful if all warring between nations
would cease, or if people would just stop being so mean.
But world peace ain't goin' to happen, not as long as men run the show.
It's obvious women have a bit more sense.
On television we watch tension mounting and exchanges blow by blow.
Peace is now spoken of in the past tense!
So what I want for Christmas, and I must warn you not to laugh,
and I know it won't dispel warring or hate
and I want the whole caboodle, not a piece or even half,
In my Christmas stocking this year,
I want to find Bill Gates!

Florence Broomfield

CHRISTMAS BELLS

Hear the bells of Christmas chime
Heralding the Child is born.
Hear on high the angels sing
On yet another Christmas morn.

Two thousand years and more have gone,
And still on Earth the people sing
Carols to commemorate
The birth of Jesus Christ, our King.

Over this war-torn world of ours
The Christmas bells again will chime
With joyful sound that brings once more
Hope of peace at Christmas time.

Barbara Dunning

GOD BLESS YE MERRY GENTLEMEN

God bless ye merry gentlemen, I say all the ladies too,
She's in the kitchen with all the work to do.
Not the merry gentleman, the lazy so and so,
The lady has the hassle, dashing to and fro.
Cleaning, shopping, the cooking to do
Not the merry gentlemen, they haven't got a clue.
Ladies buy, the Christmas gifts galore,
Not ye merry gentlemen, to them it's such a bore.
Christmas Day arrives filled with lots of cheer
While she cooks the dinner, he has a glass of beer.
After dinner he sits, perched in front of the telly
Arms folded neatly, over a bulging belly.
He snoozes all through the Queen's speech
Never thinks of the tea towel that's within easy reach.
Dishes washed, neatly put away
Time to relax after such a busy day.
About 6pm the gentlemen arise
They want their tea now, and a few mince pies.
She hands over turkey sandwiches, on a laden plate,
Gasps as the food disappears, at an alarming rate.
He goes to bed early, tired out from the day's pace
Ladies smile indulgently, or is it a grimace on their face.
To all ye merry gentlemen, to you all good night, God bless,
Without your help at Christmas, we ladies would be in a mess.

Patricia Whorwood

A SPECIAL DAY

Christmas Day in our house, it doesn't seem that long ago.
When we saw babies with angel faces.
It's been so nice to watch them grow.
Bells will ring out in Bethlehem on this very
Special day, for a baby who lay in a manger,
On a bed that was made of hay, his home was not a
Castle. We never did pretend, he brought us peace and
Happiness, we hope it will never end.

Richard Mahoney

UNTITLED

The one star that's bright over Christmas night
And that's the Lord's star.
It shines so brightly over the world
He who brings so much, if you let Him into your life.

He's kind and gentle
He watches over you, and keeps you safe and happy.
You can talk to Him anywhere
He loves you more than you'll ever know.

He watches and listens every day of your life
On this Earth, one day we celebrate His birthday.
One day we share with Him, the rest of the year He gives us.
So happy birthday Jesus and may we rest in Your bosom.

D Storey

THE CHRISTMAS SPIRIT

The Christmas spirit is sacred and dear,
It's a time to remember, a time of good cheer,
It's not the food, the parties, the drinks,
But how a man feels, the way that he thinks.

It's not decorations or expensive gifts,
But the kind thought, the word that uplifts,
It's not a time to grab and to get,
But the joy of caring, the sharing as yet.

It's the pleasure of giving to those who have not,
Rekindling through cards the love some forgot,
It's a time to remember humanity is one,
To make a child smile when war's over and done.

To bring warmth to the lonely, the widow, the poor,
The sick and the orphan, a blessing for sure,
A time to draw closer to family and friends,
May each day be Christmas, for love never ends.

Emmanuel Petrakis

FOOD FOR THOUGHT

Holly and mistletoe, tinsel and fun,
Christmas trees, baubles and more,
Mother has baked the pies and cakes,
Is there enough, or should she bake more?

It's Christmas again,
The time of year when we buy presents galore,
A jumper for Dad,
Is it his size?
Will this perfume be right for Aunt Maude?

John wants a bike, Mary a doll,
Do its eyes open and close?
Is the fifteen pound turkey cooked tender or dry?
Buy good tights for Granny, fine hose.

The shops are all bursting with all we require
To make Yuletide go with a swing,
Carols are sung in melodious tone,
The bank balance looks a bit thin.

We will cope with card writing, overnight guests,
Almost all the season entails,
But if two thousand years ago Jesus hadn't been born,
We wouldn't have Christmas today.

Dorothy M Mitchell

CHRISTMAS MIRACLE

The poor old
man had
travelled
many days
and walked
with shoulders hunched, his head bent low against
the cruel wind and driving snow. His face was deeply
lined, with beard of grey, coarse hair now white with
snow, brown teeth decayed. Tired, faltering footsteps
made his progress
slow, as he sought
for shelter from the
icy cold, somewhere
his weary body he
could lay. At last
he found the stable,
went inside and with
folk and animals
he rested there. He
woke with kings,
poor shepherds,
Hosts on High,
beheld the Christ
child in a manger
there. Tears of joy
had washed the
blindness from
his eyes and he
thanked God for
his sight with
Christmas
prayers.

Pauline Phillips

CASH CASH CASH CASH

What does Christmas mean?
Why do we celebrate?
A baby was born
Long, long ago.
We sing carols,
Buy presents galore,
We eat, drink to excess,
Have drunken arguments.
Where is the love? It's
Gimme, gimme, gimme,
He or she only gave me . . .
Next year I'll give them less.
How about the baby who
Lived and died for us,
It's Christmas,
His birthday,
Do all celebrate
His
Life?

A P Walsh

THE WONDER OF CHRISTMAS

Christmas time is here again,
Bringing joy and laughter to all men,
The birds have flown, the trees are bare,
While Jack Frost leaves a chill in the air.

The decorations twinkle bright,
Lighting up the dark of night,
Stockings hanging in a row,
Waiting for Santa Claus to show.

Children happy, they can't wait,
Leaving cookies out on the plate,
Cuddling up in their bed,
Waiting for the man in red.

Christmas morning, children will see
All the presents under the tree,
Lots of fun, lots of joy,
For every little girl and boy.

Jacqueline Anderson

THE GIFT

Up in the stable roof so high
A spider watched with beady eye
A baby in a box he did spy
I wonder, thought he, *just why*

Gifts were brought, so many
Shepherds and a little lamb
Kings with riches uncanny
The stable they did cram

Septimus, he was that spider
He'd nothing at all to give
He felt a real outsider
Just then his brain began to weave

This spider spun a web so wild
It covered right across the crib
No dust can fall upon the child
This was his gift, small but glib

His giving, small was really good
Septimus smiled just where he stood

Erica Menzies

STREET SONG
(A Christmas Carol)

'Away in a manger,
No crib for a bed'
I haven't a pillow
To rest my poor head;
Nobody cares if I
Lie here and die,
The world is my home,
And my roof is the sky;
The elements toss me
From pillar to post,
But uncaring people,
They hurt me the most;
Because I am shabby,
My clothes are unkempt,
They treat me with scorn,
With their looks of contempt;
They know not the reasons,
They know not my sorrow,
I've suffered today,
And I'm dreading tomorrow;
As they rush on their way,
And turn a blind eye,
Nobody cares if
I live or I die;
'Away in a manger,
No crib for a bed,'
I pray by tomorrow
That I will be dead.

Dorothy Neil

CHRISTMAS EVE

Silently, as the world awaits His coming,
    I gaze upwards in the nocturnal stillness
to the heavenly heights,
    where twinkling lights lustrously glow
on this hallowed, frosty winter's night.
What mystery! What wonderment!
Will I see that guiding star which leads to Bethlehem,
    that drew travellers from afar?
Vainly I search, focusing only on infinity, yet in
    my heart I know that He is there,
watching, waiting to be received.

Come Lord Jesus into this manifestly materialistic world;
come, joyful and triumphant
    into the hearts of all Your people,
rich and poor of every nation.
Come, let us celebrate Your birth and rejoice!

Malcolm F Andrews

CHRISTMAS DINNER

Christmas dinner 1973,
Mum, Nan and Grand', Gill, Steve and me.
Usual routine, I was on sprouts,
Steve was on mint sauce and Gill was dodging clouts.
Nan and Grand' like fire irons sat silent, steely, cold,
Amid swirling ghostly faces from tobacco newly rolled.
We had no record player to drown the soundless din,
Just an orchestra of pots and pans and hot fat sizzling.
At last we took our places, best china, best clothes, best day!
But no toasts to the past or the future,
And we'd long since forgotten to pray.
See, two wars and a lifetime of hardship
Had drained Nan and Grand' like the rest,
They'd forgotten their dreams and given up hopes,
Never moaned, just got through, did their best.
I think they both knew that we loved them,
Though to say so was *not* the done thing.
But Christmas dinner meant being together
And that's worth remembering.

Hilary Keating

SITTING BY THE FIRE ONE CHRISTMAS EVE

Sitting by the fire this Christmas Night,
The glowing embers are such a sight,
They crackle and dance with great alarm,
But they will never do you harm,
If you are guarded by a fireguard.
The dancing flame through children's eyes,
Will bring great joy and much surprise,
For goodness reigns in the hearts of all,
This Christmas time it makes a call.
A present for Auntie and Uncle too
Will show that you are good and true.
Your words, your bond of Christmas cheer,
May it so happen through all the year.

M Delver

DEAR SANTA

While you're helped by gnomes and elves
All that we've got is ourselves!
So when you're soaring through the skies
Replete with sherry and mince pies,
Remember Mum and Dad below,
Who work so hard that you may go
Waving, cheery in your sleigh.
Lucky sod. You get away.
When we've drunk the loyal cup
We have to do the washing up!

Mummy and me
We play with the kids round the Christmas tree.
Bounce the baby on our knee,
Again wash dishes after tea,
Prepare for guests' festivity,
Open bottles endlessly
And when the last guest finally
Makes up his fuddled mind to flee
Who does the cleaning up?

Vincent McTigue

A MERRY CHRISTMAS

A merry Christmas is full of good cheer,
When the cold nights come, we get out the beer.
Into the fire the poker will go
And when it gets red hot on it we blow
Then carefully sticking it in the glass
It's then the beer begins to bubble and splash.
Fender Ale, we used to love it
But sometimes we'd end up in a lot of trouble.
Four pints I'll drink of that tonight
And by God I'll go out like a light -
Then all of a sudden the hooter goes,
How did I know I'd fall asleep in my clothes?
I jump up quick, run as fast as I can
But alas the gaffer is closing the gate.
'I warned you last night, you'd sleep in late
But all you wanted to do was to sit by the grate
Sticking the poker in your beer,
And now you've found out it's cost you dear.
I'm docking an hour's pay.'
'And a merry Christmas to you,' I say.

Patricia Muldoon

UNTITLED

Christmas is for the children, so the people say.
They don't believe the message of that first Christmas Day.

The babe born in a manger to live His life on Earth,
Born in a lowly stable to give us second birth.

The shepherds and the wise men travelled from afar,
They knew that special baby could be found beneath the star.

The tinsel and the presents are for most the Christmas season,
But we believe that Jesus is the reason for the season.

He came to live the perfect life as it was prophesied,
And then as God had planned, He hung upon the cross and died.

His work was done, He rose again, God's work was now complete
And now our Saviour waits for us to bow down at His feet.

Just put your trust in Him, who came to save your soul and mine,
And you will have forgiveness and a wonderful Christmas time.

Linda McQueen

WHAT LOVE BRINGS

The magical charm Christmas brings,
Cannot be found in summer or in spring,
But as November leaves with its darkness and cold winter days,
Up springs December with forthcoming brighter days.
Out come the cards to send far and near,
Decorations, Christmas presents, puddings and cakes,
                                    for everyone dear.
People are busy and move to and fro,
And on people's faces it's already beginning to show.
The children prepare, and try to be good,
For Santa does not come unless you are good.
Yes something does happen on Christmas Day,
For Jesus was born, and gave us love on His birthday.

E W O'Brien

CHRISTMAS CHEER

The half moon is shining on high,
The bright stars light up the sky,
A little robin lands to enjoy another berry,
And all around the people are merry.

Christmas trees make the houses bright,
'Santa, please stop,' says the sign by the light.
Children have taken flight to their beds,
Mother keeps an eye on the weary little heads.
Mr Snowman is stood near the front door,
And inside, the heat makes another Christmas card
                                        slip to the floor.

The turkey is being cooked steady,
Crackers and presents got ready,
Excitement is all around,
And snow is now thick on the ground,
Dad's mince pies and port are found.

Morning has come and it's Christmas joy,
Children are keen to play with new toy,
However, 'tis to church we must go to pray,
To give thanks to Lord Jesus for the Saviour's day.
Bells are ringing,
Choirboys are singing,
Let this Christmas be full of good cheer,
May good will and peace, continue all year.

Daniel P Dougherty

TURKEY TIKKA MASSALA

Turkey Tikka Massala
With second helping of sprouts.
'I'm not sure about rice with stuffing,'
My Aunt Amina shouts.

Christmas time is magic
Like a full-blown
Bollywood extravaganza.
Laughter, tears, presents
And those Christmas carols,
A touch of the tragic.

We're not Christians but love the celebrations
We're hooked on the drama
Of it all.
Strategic planning in advance
Family get together
Us first, second and third generation Asians.

We mix the East with the West -
Presents, mince pies, poppadoms,
Samosas, Christmas pud, byriani
Time to reflect
Taking from each culture what we like the best.

Rather like Santa, most of us work
On that special day.
I believe that he's got Asian relations
Because despite the weather,
Working conditions -
The show must go on
Service to be offered come what may.

Fakhira Ali

CHRISTMAS

Christmas is buying food, drinks,
cards and presents.
Exhaustion.

Christmas is searching for the perfect present,
and being in six places at once.
Exhaustion.

Christmas is cooking food and writing cards
and wrapping presents.
Exhaustion.

Christmas is putting up trees, lighting lights
and decorating houses.
Excitement.

Christmas is mailing cards, waiting for the postman,
and watching TV.
Excitement.

Christmas is unwrapping presents at dawn
and watching the faces around you.
Excitement.

Christmas is eating and drinking
and being with family and friends.
Love.

Christmas is singing carols
and listening to the story of a baby just born.
Love.

Christmas is
Love.

Glenys Chapman

WHAT A WAIT

At night upon my pillow I lie
When you're in the sky, flying so high,
When Rudolph's guiding you with his red nose,
I'm tossing and turning in my bedclothes,
I shut my eyes tight and try to sleep
But I'm so excited, I'll have to peep.

He was dressed in red from head to toe,
Saying, 'Ho! Ho! Ho! And away we go!'
Down he came with a crash and a bang
While Rudolph and Prancer above him sang,
No longer looking red and bright,
But now a dirty, sooty sight.

Those reindeer were naughty, and made him tip out,
Santa was angry and started to shout,
But he's so jolly he just can't stay glum
He delivered my presents, oh Christmas is fun.

Melissa Usher (8)

CHRISTMAS IS . . .

Christmas is baubles, tinsel and trees,
Christmas is snowmen and puddles that freeze,
Christmas is turkey and plum pudding sweet,
Christmas is presents wrapped up so neat.

Christmas is candles and carollers singing,
Christmas is angels and church bells ringing,
Christmas is school and nativity plays,
Christmas is hurriedly counting the days.

Christmas is holly and mistletoe kisses,
Christmas is shopping in brightly lit cities,
Christmas is waiting for Santa to come,
Christmas is happiness, laughter and fun.

Christmas is children without any toy,
Christmas is home without any joy,
Christmas is having nothing to eat,
Christmas is having no one to greet.

Christmas is having no coat to wear,
Christmas is loneliness, cold and despair,
Christmas is drunkenness, anger and fears,
Christmas is pain, discomfort and tears.

Christmas is having nowhere to live,
Christmas is having no one to give,
Christmas is having nothing to share,
Christmas is having no one to care.

Let us remember, we who have plenty,
Let us remember the hands that are empty,
Let us remember those who reach out,
Let us remember what it's all about.

For Christmas is *Jesus,* born in a stall,
Christmas is *love,* given for all.

Ruth Martin

CHRISTMAS IN A NUTSHELL
(Or . . . A Real Christmas)

I remember Christmas when . . .
so 'n' so was with us then . . .
shopping in the driving rain.
No Christmas puddings! What a pain!
I remember Christmas past . . .
him 'n' her - they didn't last.
Remember when the tree fell down?
Uncle Jimmy! What a clown!
Jingle Bells! Jingle Bells!
Jingle all the way,
all that fuss 'n' flapping over . . .
just another day.
Captured in a photograph
silly hats and smiles.
People round your table
have travelled, miles and miles . . .
Jingle Bells! Jingle Bells!
Jingle all the dishes.
You may have fed an army, but did you feed the *fishes?*
The dogs have Christmas dinner too
and fart the night away.
We blamed the dogs, but who it was -
we really just can't say!
Jingle Bells! Jingle Bells!
Jingle all the night,
Wehey! We got through Christmas,
without a single fight!
Well . . . *almost!*

Carol & Katie Leadbetter

LIGHT OF THE WORLD

L ord, Your light has shone into our humble lives
I shall light up the Lord's everlasting candle
G lowing Jesus, like a torch which does not run out
H is love is a flickering fire
'T is a twinkling star in the sky

O xygen which He provides
F ireworks which explode in the night sky

T ouch of light that you can see in the starlight
H allelujah! Seeing the blazing colours in Jesus' fire
E ndless love and light

W orld that the sun shines upon
O pen darkness which has been turned into light
R eflection from the light into the water
L ightning which crashes in the sky
D arkness will turn to a blazing light.

April Keefe

THE MEANING OF CHRISTMAS

The scarlet berried holly bush,
Cone spruce and mistletoe.
Snug rooms bedecked with tinsel,
Log embers burning low.

Bright baubles on the Christmas tree,
Ensnare the dancing light.
Silky ribboned packages.
Precursors of delight.

Pealing bells and carollers,
Bearing lanterns all aglow.
Santa in his laden sleigh,
Skims o'er the frosted snow.

Red-breasted robin, on snowy bough.
Lone snowman standing guard.
You could also find a reindeer,
On your pretty Christmas card.

Many things can be depicted,
In this season of good cheer,
But what does Christmas really mean?
The truth may bring a tear.

'Twas long ago in Bethlehem
Three kings came from afar,
To a lowly stable, cold and bare,
Beneath their guiding star.

Jesus Christ, our Saviour,
Was born to us on Earth.
This little child, was God's own Son.
We celebrate His birth.

Lucy Ann Timmins

A Child Became A Man

On the Earth from up above
Came a gift full of love
Found a gift we love the most
Sent by Father, Son and Holy Ghost
But the gift become just as one
Just a child sent as God's son
Now this child we have found
To walk with Him, hand in hand
The proof of this is found on shore
Free of sin, we have no more
By the waters, hand in hand
Full of grace as on the sand
The prints are there for all to see
The cross, the sign on Calvary
The child is a child no more
But a man, all our sins He bore
His body broken for you and me
To be with Him in all eternity

W N Brown

COLD WINTER NIGHTS

Cold winter nights we would retire
to sit huddled close around the fire.
Eating our toast and drinking our tea
as warm and cosy as can be.

The warmth from the fire
the coal reflecting a glow.
Watching through the window
as people struggle home in the snow.

We were all together, so safe and secure,
warmth and love all around, of that I was so sure.
These are all my memories of Christmas yesteryear,
memories so precious, I hold them very dear.

My mother and father, the providers of this pleasure
created these memories which I have to treasure.
So just remember when Christmas comes again,
enjoy sharing time with family, even if it is a pain.

My parents are no longer here
not long passed, way up high.
But the memories they've left me
no millionaire could buy.

T E Smith

CHRISTMAS

I always thought that Christmas time
Was a time for love and giving,
And a time to thank the Lord above
For the joy of simply living.

But all I seem to hear these days
Is - 'Can I have?' and 'Oh, I want!'
With tantrums, tears and tempers,
If they're simply told, 'You can't!'

Where did being grateful go,
For the smaller things in life?
When did we stop asking for a world,
That's free from strife?

I hope that we can go back soon,
Right the wrongs while we're still able.
For the one who gave us everything,
Was quite happy in a stable.

Barbara Sims

CHRISTMAS 2004

I'd rather be honest about Christmas time - mine!
Family memories not magical
Apart from when Nan was here.
Christmas was never true,
True Christmas is about love, warmth.
The lights, the smell of the pine tree.
It's about the memories of happiness.
This Christmas was different, there's no other word,
I didn't stay with they family as they didn't want me there.
I was alone, but felt at peace.
I'm being true to myself and foremost
Welcomed by a friend I never knew existed until now.
I realise the true meaning of Christmas 2004.
Friends are our chosen family, life moves on.
The spirit of Christmas present, has set me free.

Laura A Sadler

The Magic Of Santa

Time passes swiftly by us
And Christmas time draws near,
We hear the sound of laughter,
Of merriment and cheer.

Whilst all of this is happening
In a land so far away,
The snow is falling softly, as we wait for Christmas Day.

It is in this land of magic, that there lives a gentle soul,
Who is preparing hard for a journey far
From this land called the North Pole.

His aim is to target children with a gentle, caring love
And to brightly light their faces up
Like the stars that shine above

So as Christmas morning meets us
And carols we gaily sing
When we open all our presents
And we hear the church bells ring.

Let us stop for just one second,
Some time we all can take
To think of all those children
Who Santa couldn't make.

Let us take a look into the sky
At the star, lighting above,
And make a wish for children
A new year filled with love.

Lynn Marie Boyle

UNTITLED

In a stable far away,
A baby born on Christmas Day,
Shepherds gathered around to pray,
Kings brought great gifts of splendour.

Angel's voices filled the air, singing
'Gloria in Excelsis
Novus Rex Natus'
From that day forth, the world was saved.

Today to celebrate we hang
Decorations, trees and carnations.
Children's eyes open wide with glee
Presents scattered around a tree,
Jesu Christus et Magister.

M C Taylor

CHRISTMAS BELONGS TO EVERYONE

They say this time is for children
It's true, as I've been there before
It was long ago, it was Neverland
I haven't been there since

The magic of the fantasy
That filled my mind and soul
And I truly believed that elves were nearby
Who read my list from the chimney

The astonishment of the moment
Seeing an empty plate and glass
And looking for the slightest hint of trickery
But no, he had really been to my house

I would shiver in the night air
No central heating then
But shivered too with excitement
At the presents 'round my bed

Crisp air, pine, a smoking fire
Sage and onion, tangerines
Pulled crackers, chocolate, Mum's Soir de Paris
A pot pourri of magic smells
The best could ever be

Memories so fond and dear
And many more so vivid
As much as I love them, I wish I could find
Others to take their place

I long for that magic to behold
When and where did it go -
Did I lose it, was it taken?
Did it die, who stole my Christmas?
I want it back again!

If I can learn the lesson of a child
To believe that magic does exist
And see through their eyes
The wonder of the great story
The fun of Christmas Day games
The belief that I need to be good
Or carrots and coal would be the result.

Christmas may be for children
But the magic is there to be shared
If you can see and behold as a child, once again
You'll be reconciled to the wonder of Christmas
Believe me, it's still there.

Meryl Kelbrick

WILL CHRISTMAS BE WHITE?

'Will Christmas be white?'
Ask anxious small children,
The morning brings frost
But no snow is in sight.

They busy themselves
With presents and sweets,
Unwrapping and clapping
The gifts and the treats.

Snowflakes like goose down
Drift silently earthwards,
Footsteps are muffled
By the street's new white gown.

One shriek through the night
Alerts every small child,
This feast day is perfect
This Christmas *is* white!

Meg Fraser

UNTITLED

Christmas time for boys and girls
To get the toys they want
Christmas tree and fairy lights
Fun and games, without the fights
Only fun and laughter
Is all that really matters
A time for friends and family
To show they really care
And remind us all the meaning
That Jesus Christ was born.

Christmas time to many
Means lots of food and drink
It would be nice if only
They took the time to think
There are lots of old and lonely
Who would love to be cared and thought about
So take the time and stop awhile
As one day it may well be
A nan or gramps or mum or dad
Or maybe even me.

Sylvia Green

INSPIRATION

On a cold night of Christmas
I lay awake
in anticipation of daybreak

At Heaven's early rise
my favourite alone time
I heard a winter call
a bluebird and a demon
all in one.
A blue-chested robin
heralding the morn

Oh winged Santa Claus
singing me a gift, dressed in song
a vision of the dawning
or Heaven's rift
winter gone

Osita Nwankwo

IT'S CHRISTMAS TIME ONCE AGAIN

It's Christmas time once again
snow on the ground.
When the hedgehogs hibernate,
not one to be found.

It's also Christmas for your pets,
however big or small.
But remember the lonely ones,
that have no home at all.

The homeless people on the streets,
alone in the dark,
nothing else to do
but hang around the park.

The kids are excited,
leaving Santa a mince pie.
While their parents run around
looking for presents to buy.

The baubles hanging up
and presents under the tree.
The lights around the window,
for everyone to see.

The snowmen, holly,
robins and reindeer,
Then it's all over,
until next year.

Emma Cardwell

DEAR SANTA

Dear Santa with your beard so white
Are you getting ready for your journey tonight?
Dear Santa with your suit so red
Are you making sure that all children are in bed?
Dear Santa with your cheeks so flushed
Please don't end up in another rush!
Dear Santa with your little button nose
My dad said, 'Please don't set off the garden hose.'
Dear Santa with your sleigh so high
You come but once a year, and all I ask is why?
Dear Santa with your elves working hard
My mum said, 'Please don't let the reindeers go to the toilet
                                              in our yard.'
Dear Santa at last I know what I will be getting
And please don't go on your way, forgetting
That I want surprises on Christmas Day
With my great big smile, as I shout, 'Hooray!'

Bethany Sloan

THE CHRISTMAS BUILD-UP

I can feel that Christmas is in the air,
There's decorations everywhere.
The kids have all gone shopping mad,
In search of presents for Mum and Dad.

Santa's in his Grotto with his reindeers and elves,
People think there's a food war on,
They've emptied all the shelves.
I go to buy a turkey, there's not one left in sight.
I should have listened to my mum. I know she's always right.

I wake up in the morning, the snow is crisp and white,
The kids are so excited, they didn't sleep all night.
And now it's time to sit and eat and enjoy our Christmas Day,
And watch the happy faces as the children sit and play.

Avril Vormawah

WHAT DOES CHRISTMAS MEAN TO YOU?

What does Christmas mean to you
If anything at all?
Maybe decorations bright
That lighten up the hall.

Maybe a Christmas party
With food and drink galore,
Or holiday in Cyprus
Or other foreign shore.

Perhaps it speaks of presents
All wrapped beneath a tree,
Or maybe turkey dinner
And nap on the settee.

Or time to think of others
Who died in the past year,
With sadness and confusion
And shedding of a tear.

Is it just another day
Upon the street outside?
Cold and hungry, friendless too,
Nowhere to go inside.

He whose name the season takes
Was born in stable bare.
He came to Earth with nothing,
He came to show His care.

Whate'er you think of Christmas,
Whatever you may do,
Seek out the Christ of Christmas
And find His love for you.

Malcolm Evans

CHRISTMAS COMES BUT ONCE A YEAR

Christmas comes but once a year
With love and warmth and lots of good cheer
The house is lit with bright coloured lights
That dangle and swing from dangerous heights

The Christmas tree stands tall in the corner
With tinsel and baubles draped to adorn her
The presents are placed with care and attention
For little tots' fingers to prod with affection

The cupboards are full of pickles and puddings
There's just no more room for anymore tins
The Bramleys and Brussels are stacked in the shed
This is surely the time when we're all over-fed!

But love it or hate it, there's one thing for sure
Christmas is good at making us poor
So enjoy the festivities with all you hold dear
And start saving hard for Christmas next year!

Christine Shelley

CHRISTMAS IS COMING

'Christmas is coming
The goose is getting fat'
So goes the old song
Sounding rather pat.
But what about the people
Who will not have a dinner?
What about the millions
Daily growing thinner?
Do we just forget them
Whilst we drink and eat?
Do we send them money
Or something for their feet?
What a world we live in
Where thousands have to die
Because some others want to fight.
Can you fathom why?

Judith Hinds

TO MUM AND DAD

It's Christmas Eve
Time for bed
Because Santa is riding on his sled
Snuggled up, fast asleep
There is no sound, not even a peep

Rudolf is guiding the way
All the presents piled on his sleigh
Down the chimney with his sack
And at the end is a delicious snack
It may be whisky or some wine
It's so lovely at Christmas time

Oliver Povey (11)

CHRISTMAS PRESSURE

Christmas carols filled the air and bright lights set the scene
Shop windows filled with goodies and glitz, the best there's ever been
All entice to buy, buy, buy and spend your money here
To ride the wave of a spending spree for Christmas and New Year
But for Emma Smith this time of year, was full of fear and dread
She needed money for presents and her children needed to be fed
With the pressure from her children and the lure of tinselled shops
Once again on a tiny wage, she would put out all the stops
The children wanted branded goods, mobile phones with famous names
All their mates had computers and things with lots and lots of games
As Christmas neared, the pressure grew and so did the sleepless nights
Many tears hidden from her children, amid the bright tree lights
Some presents she bought on credit, others by shopping around
In cheaper shops and market stalls, for bargains to be found
Then to pay for the Christmas food, the rent would not be paid
She would worry in the weeks to come and a payment offer made
Christmas morning came at last and Emma watched in fear
As the children opened their presents, she hid away a tear
But tears turned into smiles and fears were overcome
As they both jumped up upon her knee saying,
'Thanks, we love you Mum.'

Bill Dooley

I Sent A Letter To Santa

I like how it happens when the weather gets cold
And sometimes my mum says, it even snows.
So that people go out and skate and play
Perhaps I can do that, but not today.
I sent off my letter to Santa, Mum helped
I might soon get better and go skating myself
But for now I must stay indoors in my bed
With Teddy and Bunny to talk to instead.
When Daddy comes home, we will have a nice hug
And I'll have cocoa at bedtime in my special mug.
I have to get better for Christmas Day
Cos Nanny and Grandad are coming to stay.
Daddy said Santa brings lovely new toys
To all the good little girls and boys
So I am trying and trying to be extra good
So he'll send me a present like Dad said he would.

Norma Griffiths

CHRISTMAS IMAGES

The pink-blue sky of morning
White frost upon the ground
The playing of Christmas carols
Happiness all around

Sweet smiles on children's faces
The aroma of pine needles in the air
Pealing of the church bells
Signalling a time for thanks in prayer

Feasting on the turkey
Feeling stuffed from Christmas pud
Playing board games with the children
Drinking more than you should

Hats and decorations
Wrapping paper on the floor
Kissing under the mistletoe
A wreath upon the door

All the images of Christmas
The fun, the laughter, the care
I send the blessings of the season
To everyone, everywhere.

Karen Giles

THE CHRISTMAS STORY

The skies were filled with angels
Who sang of the Saviour's birth
The shepherds came rushing to see Him
And worshipped Jesus, the creator of Earth
That night they were so excited
As they talked of the sight they had seen
Gathering their sheep, home they hurried
For their wives wouldn't believe where they'd been
Then later came the wise travellers
For miles they had followed the star
No ordinary child had been born here
For He also had travelled from afar
They laid down their gifts of splendour
Frankincense, myrrh and some gold
There they knelt in awe and wonder
Before this child, whose birth the prophets foretold
Now two thousand years later, we should still consider this child
No longer the babe in the manger, lying there so meek and mild
For Jesus grew up, doing the will of His Father
Even though a cruel cross was His aim
Submission to this, He would rather
Than condemn all mankind to Hell's flame
And so at this Christmas season
As the nativity of Our Lord we celebrate
May we all not forget the real reason
And give God the praise for He's great
Why not give some time to say thank you
For coming, that first Christmas time
Joining angels and shepherds and wise men too
And worship Jesus, God's Son divine.

Rebecca Walker

A SPECIAL CHILD

A long time ago
In a land far away,
A child, He was born,
Who is still remembered today.

Not in a hospital
And not in a bed,
But in a manger
He laid His sweet head.

This child, He was special,
Sent from above.
That even all the animals
Came to show their love.

To stand around the manger,
They all came to see
That this special child
Was born for you and me.

And above the manger
Set on a hill,
A bright star it shone
That still shines still.

It pointed to where
The sweet child lay,
So three wise men
Could travel to pray.

The child had a name,
That is well known to us,
And that wonderful name
Is the Lord Jesus.

John Morris

PANS HITTING THE LINOLEUM
AND OTHER PANDEMONIUM

The stuffing's on the ceiling
The plate's in bits on the floor
The phone in the hall is ringing out
And the guests have arrived at the door

The roasties are a bit too crisp
The dog's got his teeth in the pudding
My headache's no longer a very slight pain
But an intermittent thudding

Even the turkey's had enough
It's got up and flown away
The mobile's run out of credit
So I can't ring the takeaway

So what will I do with these twenty-five guests
I'll ply them with lots of fine wine
Then lead them all round to the local pub
Where we'll have Christmas dinner in style

Paula Larkin

CHILDHOOD MEMORIES

Pears and ribbons, girlish visions
remind me of a childhood past.
This at last, the day is nearing,
and I'm clearing the snow from
the footpath away.

Bright lights and sleepless nights,
in anticipation of what Santa's given,
to all good children, parcels
and packets, table-tennis racquets.

A choir is singing, bringing cheer
on a winter's day, tinsel and
baubles, the cold wind blowing
the cobwebs away.

Susan Byers

THE REASON WE HAVE CHRISTMAS

Amidst the flurry of presents and food,
Drinking and eating, then sleeping it off,
The reason for Christmas is somehow lost.
When the wonderment of Christmas Day is over,
Do we stop and think why we had what we had today?
We all are so ready to eat, drink and be merry, as we should.
But laying in a manger far away, in a land far off,
Was the Virgin Mary who gave birth to a little boy,
Named Jesus.
He too had presents from three wise men, who came to
Honour Him.
Now the wonderment of Christmas Day is over once more,
Gone until this time next year, when we all start again.
Mary had a baby boy in a stable, lowly and cold, so we can
Celebrate the time we know as 'Christmas'.

Terri Granger

SEVEN DAYS TO CHRISTMAS

Seven days to go,
Seasonal monsoon weather, shopping at its peak,
Late hour frantics that best-ever present seek.
Office parties are the vogue, an elephantine trap,
Too much to drink, your friends and colleagues clap.

Six days to go,
Buy cheap, buy twice, the Christmas lights have failed,
Brown needles everywhere, except upon senescent tree.
Forgotten first time cards still to write and be mailed.
Butcher rings to say he's lost *our* bronze designer turkey.

Five days to go,
Cancel Christmas, the twins just vomit and have spots,
Advice Line says don't bath them, keep them cool.
Burn two dozen mince pies, too many sherry tots,
Discover burgled chocolate box, feel such a silly fool.

Four days to go,
Threaten kids with ghastly sanctions, know I'm wrong,
Bedrooms tidied, silence reigns, no last year's toys in sight,
Aunts and uncles, annual in-laws *'just drop in'* but stay too long,
Sweet talk and knowing glances from the offspring reason things alright

Three days to go,
It's nearly midnight when I leave dishevelled store
With trolley overladen, my body clock reversed,
I zigzag past the hardy songsters frozen to the core,
Thrusting tins and singing songs so many years rehearsed.

Two days to go,
The kids behave like angels, well beyond my wishes
Two moons now since last fight, twelve hours to another night.
Hair brushed, teeth cleaned, volunteers even for the dishes,
I'm already washed out and wince at mirror's sight.

One day to go,
My patience has absconded along with seasonal goodwill,
I'm irritable and nervous in case *my* stocking Santa doesn't fill.
So I get lessons in behaviour from wary Dan and wily Harri
Even though I'm sixty-five and they're just a knowing *three!*

Mike Hayes

WINTERTIME

Christmas is in wintertime.
Why did God's son come in a cold clime?
It was to warm our hearts, to bring some cheer,
To have His birthday this time of year!
Our world can be a hostile place,
God came to Earth, so full of grace.
There are places in our world today,
With no room for people with nothing to pay!
Some people have no family to give cheer,
No money to spend on things that are dear!
They see the rich spending and feel sad,
No wonder they think Christmas is bad!
We hope the goodwill in people's hearts today,
Will think of the homeless and those with no money to pay!
There are also those living alone,
They see people going to parties while they stay at home.
At this time, the elderly are afraid to go out,
So many robberies, and pavements are slippy when they go about.
We hope to be positive and try to see good things,
And bring hope to others in the time God brings.
We can look forward to the months ahead,
And bring happiness to others in situations of dread.
May God help us in wintertime.
In a dark, cold world, let His light shine.

J Hallifield

DON'T INVITE THEM DEAR!

M ust we have them around this year?
E ating our mince pies and drinking my beer
R uining our peace with their blooming toys
R unning around like typical boys
Y apping and yawning, oh what a noise!

C ouldn't we make some excuse?
H ow about chickenpox for a ruse?
R emember last year they bought me a tie
I t was bright yellow, not pleasing to the eye
S aid I liked it, had to tell a lie
M aybe we should just put on the charm
A fter all, it's Christmas and it won't do much harm
S ometimes we have to put on the charm!

Peter G H Payne

PEACE AT CHRISTMAS

Gift wrapped parcels beneath the tree,
Children gathered round Santa's knee.
Shimmering stars, shiny and bright,
Carols drift through the silent night.
The Earth is at peace 'neath the virgin snow,
As the moon alone casts its eerie glow,
And as dawn breaks on a new tomorrow,
Let's hope for a world without pain and sorrow.

Susie Field

MERRY CHRISTMAS

M ince pies, iced cake and sausage rolls
E aten only out of duty.
R ather too much wine is taken
R aucous laughter with deadpan eyes
Y ou'll regret it in the morning.

C arols from Kings again last night
H erald angels, shepherds watching
'R ather hackneyed,' Grandpa mumbles
'I liked it!' barked his second wife.
S omeone's broken the Christmas lights.
T empers darken with the evening
M other's screaming at Auntie Sue
A nd Father slams another door.
S omewhere there's a Merry Christmas?

Patricia Smith

THOUGHTS FOR SANTA

Dear Santa, you should see our Christmas tree,
It has fairy lights and baubles bright,
Mummy says I have to write and
Let you know what to bring me on Christmas night.

I would like lots of racing cars, and
A track to race them on, with flags and stars,
My favourite though would be a red fire engine,
So could you see your way to bring me one?

Mummy says I've not to be greedy,
Cos there's lots of children poor and needy,
I'll say a prayer Santa on Christmas night,
So you bring a little happiness to their plight.

Thank you Santa for reading this letter,
Our Lord Jesus was born to make this world better,
So on Christmas Eve when we say our prayers,
We ask the adults for safety, love and care.

Elizabeth Hiddleston

OUR CHRISTMAS SONNET 2004

Our warm home is a real joy to behold,
Our Christmas tree is small, but with good cheer,
Decorations, cards from friends, new and old,
Baubles and all, they come out ev'ry year.
With family and friends, we have enough,
So good food, wine and gifts, let us then share,
The lonely, the sad and sick find it tough,
We took hampers to ill folk, bringing cheer.
At midnight Mass, the faithful sang with love,
Carols, choir and incense praise the Above,
Good tidings we bring, so let us rejoice.
I was ill with cancer two years ago,
Now married and healthy, I love life so.

Mary May Robertson

CHRISTMAS

The holly and the mistletoe
the warmth of love and winter snow.
The family that's set apart, but brought
together with the heart.
The age old sound of church bells ringing,
choir boys and carol singing.
And just for one day a year,
a whole world full of Christmas cheer.

Shirley Parker

A SHORT LETTER TO SANTA

Throughout our lives we have eagerly awaited
Your visit to us on Christmas Eve,
From childhood to manhood, all have remained
Eager to see whether our requests we receive.
From time to time our requests have floundered
As we ask for an item quite over the top,
And then disappointment reduces our pleasure
And faith in Santa Claus begins to flop.
In adulthood we try once more to enthuse
To our children the idea that Santa Claus
Will try and produce all their requests -
But instil they must be sensible of course.
So Santa, now we give thanks for the years
When a happy Christmas to us has been given,
And now as a senior citizen we give praise
And thanks to the one true Santa - our Father in Heaven.

Jean C Pease

CHRISTMAS EVE

Oh! I am so excited, it's Christmas Eve again
lying in my little bed looking through the windowpane,
The night is clear and frosty, as I look at the starry sky
I saw a sleigh and reindeer, silently go by.
I clapped my hands in sheer delight
will I ever get to sleep tonight?
My heart nearly skips a beat,
was that the sound of reindeer feet?
I wonder if he'll stop or not,
was that a noise on the chimney pot?
I close my eyes and pretend to sleep,
I'm so excited I have to peep.
Was that a scrape on the bedroom floor
or was it a creak of my bedroom door?
Oh yes, I'm so excited,
there's nothing like Christmas Eve.
Waiting for dear old Santa, but you really must believe.
I've left mince pies for Santa
and carrots for his reindeer team.
This night is filled with magic
or is it all a dream?

Mike Harrison

A CHRISTMAS WISH

I looked up at the sky
and saw a shining star
I wondered if you saw it too
in your land afar
And did we wish the same thing
and hope that it comes true
I hope you wished the same as me
peace for me and you.

And as the starlight faded
in the night-time sky aglow
And Christmas morn began to dawn
and it began to snow
It brought us peace
and war did cease
Oh on that Christmas Day
and everyone was happy
in a world that's gone astray

Babies crying and children sighing
with happiness and joy
Presents round the Christmas tree
for every girl and boy
No hate, no bombs, no guns, no knives,
no suffering, no war
This was our wish for Christmas
today and evermore.

Wendy Keenan

THE MAGIC OF CHRISTMAS

All the shops are full of glitter,
There are gifts and toys galore;
Tinsel and bright lights appear
And weary spirits soar.
So many people crowd around
To spend their hard earned cash,
Rushing here and everywhere -
Their lives just one mad dash!

Much food and drink upon the shelves
(Inviting folk to buy),
Yule logs, puddings, Christmas cakes
There to attract the eye;
And all along the busy streets,
The Christmas lights just glow,
As the shoppers mingle there
The joyful minutes flow.

But does the magic disappear
Once Christmas Day has passed?
Is that what it's all about -
Is everyone downcast?
For it's a costly Christmas
The world enjoys today,
With its deep, true meaning
Oft lost along the way.

For real Christmas is for sharing
The precious love and care,
Which God has gifted to us
A present, pure and rare.
For Jesus came at Christmas
Such joy and peace to bring,
So let us now remember.
Let us His praises sing.

Anne Gray

TRUE SPIRIT OF CHRISTMAS

Christmas time does come but once a year
But from August you know that it's here
When shopping you may then start to see
Many different presents for you and for me
Christmas can sometimes be a time of cheer
With ones you love being so near

However if Christmas is a time you dread
And bold steps you always fear to tread
Remember like many times before now have shown
Many you thought were true friends have flown
Try seeing it this way; you've been freed
From those with a motive of selfish greed

When looking at the meaning of Christmas true
What images does it conjure up to you?
Can you really remember what Christmas is about?
When society today values pure continues to flout
At times you don't feel all that strong
Remember the one who gently guides you along

As Christmas morning dawns so fresh and new
Can I ask a small favour of you?
As your turkey you do begin to savour
Don't forget who this day it does favour
At Christmas if you feel like giving in
Look to where life our Saviour did begin.

Sophia Cartland

No Christmas

Christmas became non-existent
Because Dad tripped over the bed
Drunk as a skunk he was
But I, nothing said
When he left my room
I opened all my prezzies

Played with them I did
Until sleep I needed, see
Them in the morning
11.15am I came down
Mum said, 'You're late!'
I said, 'I know!'
Wearing no frown.

Michael D Bedford

CHRISTMAS TIME

Some celebrate this time of year
In the sunshine or the snow
People from around the world
Have different ideas and beliefs for this time as we know.

Some view it as a family time
Others it brings about doubts
For some it is a hardship
As the money always runs out.

Christmas time is a holiday
Where sharing and giving is rife
A time to remember the loved ones
All the special people in one's life.

Most of all Christmas to me
Is all about family and friends
Reflecting on the year that has been
And to enjoy all the good times to the end.

Julie Banyard

A LITTLE CHRISTMAS POEM

Sticky, silver paper
Wrap the presents tight.
The decorations are all here,
Santa will come. He just might!

Lovely, juicy meat.
Everyone will feast.
Congratulations to the cook
Let's carve the roast, beast!

Screaming, excited kids
Run round and round the tree.
What presents will they get?
Only Santa holds the key!

Philippa Sterritt

I REMEMBER CHRISTMAS

Looking back on childhood days,
I'd turn the hand of time,
To have again those I loved,
My granny in her prime,
She seemed so young,
I'd not believe that she would ever die.
I never thought that she'd grow old,
How fast the years went by.
Her kitchen with its gorgeous smell,
The turkey and the cake,
She made our Christmas dinner,
My gran, she loved to bake,
Christmas then, the shops so bright,
The women wearing shawls,
The market full of goodies,
The decorated stalls,
I remember childhood days,
So often I would play,
Marbles in the gutter,
Till Mum called us away.
Summer in the park we'd play,
Till darkness fell at the close of day
And sometimes our bikes we'd take,
And cycle round the boating lake.
I remember Christmas, now all I loved have gone,
I placed the holly on a grave,
For life must carry on.

Vera Parsonage

CHRISTMAS BORE!

Christmas has become a bore,
What was it like in days of yore?
What was it we all looked for?
It just ain't there, not anymore.

The bells are ringing in the spire,
The children singing in the choir.
You are sitting near a fire
Thinking soon you must retire.

Christmas is coming - what do you say?
It's only just another day.
I'm too old even to play.
Forget it - it will pass away.

Walter Dalton

CHRISTMAS

When did it fade - that haunting spell
Of myth that masked its secrets well
With magic touch of shimmering glow
In frosted light on settling snow?

When did it fade - that sense of joy
To see, gift-wrapped, the Christmas toy
With tinselled string and mistletoe
In festive sacks we treasured so?

When did it fade - the need to see
Those sparkling lights adorn the tree
Which, glimmering soft in shaded light
Bewitched our dreams on Christmas night?

Now we are old - but still the spell -
That magic touch we knew so well
Survives to haunt, entrance, ensnare
The young enchanted everywhere!

Jo Lewis

THE COST OF CHRISTMAS

I was in the shops the other week when I heard a woman say,
'I hate this time of year, you know. I'd rather go away
And spend the money on myself in some nice hot resort.
Christmas costs us far too much - just look at what I've bought!'
Well, I had a look, just nosy-like, into her shopping trolley.
Good grief! I thought, and, *Gracious me!* and, *Flipping 'eck!*
                                         and *Golly!*
I think she'd bought the whole of Tesco's superstore that day.
I don't know how she got it home or stored it all away!
There were crackers, there were presents, there was paper, tape
                                         and tags,
There was every kind of wine and beer, and fruit and nuts in bags,
There was food for forty people, at the very least, I'm sure.
No wonder Christmas costs so much and seems like such a chore!
So I thought about this lady, and what she'd done made little sense
Because Christmas shouldn't really be about the pounds and pence!
Oh, it cost enough those years ago when God first sent His Son.
I mean - He left a lot behind to be the 'Chosen One'.
He had it all up there you know, in Heaven, with His dad,
But He came down here and was born on Earth to mix in with the bad,
To show them all a way to live for other people's good,
But the powerful took exception and did all that they could
To get Him into trouble with the rulers of the day,
Who had Him nailed upon a cross - they really made Him pay!
And so the cost of Christmas is not a cost we have to meet,
For God above paid with His love, with nails through hands and feet.

Sally Drury

CHRISTMAS NIGHTMARE

Christmas is coming and I'm in a stew
Haven't got any money to spend
And I don't know what to do
All the presents the kids want, seem to cost so much
My husband says he hasn't any money
And he's left me in the lurch

What am I to do now that I'm on my own
When the kids are tucked up in bed
I'm just listening for the phone
Maybe my mum and dad will call, then come and help me out
If my ex-husband shows his face
The whole street will hear me shout

I'm hoping maybe I'll have some luck or get some extra pay
I'd love to see the kids happy
Opening their presents on Christmas Day
At this time it's only a dream, I can't see it coming true
Christmas is coming and
I don't know what to do

Christmas is here now, gone are the horrid dreams
The family's got together, it's not half as bad as it seems
Mum and Dad are here for Christmas
And everything is fine
We are all enjoying the mince pies
With a glass of Christmas wine.

Martha D'Souza

A CHRISTMAS ANNIVERSARY

Thinking back to that Christmas when we first met
A Christmas Day for sure, I will not easily forget
You looked at me and I wondered if you would talk
I liked your smile and the wiggle as you walk
So many years have we now seen
The many lands where we have been
Our children now are fully grown
Such fine seeds have we both sown
My mind goes back to that first Christmas night
What was to be was so very, very right
Never once did I set out to deceive
You can be very sure of me, just believe
That Christmas night we walked upon the sand
The first Christmas I held your hand
So long ago, in the far and distant past
What we have, will always and forever last
It has just gone midnight now, I can hear you say
Don't sleep my love for it is now Christmas Day
I had bought her flowers, such a beautiful bunch
Now we are about to have our Christmas lunch
My mind goes back to that Christmas Day we met
A day for sure I will not easily or forever 'forget'
You have given me many presents along the way
All I can give is love, on this very fine Christmas Day.

Francis McGarry

A CHRISTMAS THOUGHT

It's Christmas again once more we moan
but spare a thought for those with no home.
While we sit around a dressed Christmas tree,
open our gifts and eat our tea,
relax, get together and watch TV.
What of the homeless out on the street
cold and alone, we're unlikely to meet.
A new cardboard box - their Christmas gift;
window shop around Harrods, then they will drift.
They'll relish our leftover bin liner bags,
their treasure; our rubbish; their new clothes; our rags.
Be without family or loved ones,
we will think of those while we're having fun?
While we enjoy the Christmas time hype,
an old man, a vagrant, smokes dirt from his pipe.
As we sing carols or keep warm inside,
think of those people who live outside.

Linda Lawrence

DID YOU SEE SANTA?

Did you see Santa up in the sky
With his reindeer, flying high?
He's on his way to every child
With toys on his sled highly piled.

Looking jolly in his fur-trimmed red suit,
Could he be playing a lute?
Going to visit every house tonight
Filling children with delight.

Packages and parcels round his feet;
No doubt, even things to eat.
On the ground the snow is pristine white
Santa's got a busy night.

See the glee on the little faces
In the morning in all places.
With excitement they jump about,
But he'll leave no one without.

J Millington

CHRISTMAS CASH

Watch out for Christmas
take heed what I say,
else you will be wondering
what you did with your pay.
It creeps up and grabs you
almost like magic,
but the consequences
could be financially tragic.
The budget you promised
Christmas will break,
those limits you set
Christmas will take.
It will flutter around you
with a tempting surprise,
you won't even notice
your overdrafts rise.
Your credit card
will know no bounds,
As Christmas is full
of money-thirsty hounds.
Stick to your budget
don't let the bills mount,
after all, it's not the cost
it's the thought that counts.

Brenda Birchall

CHRISTMAS

All over England,
native trees surrender
their holly and ivy and mistletoe:
as if to pacify, in pagan ritual,
the spirits of the winter solstice.

Whilst in the northern Arctic wastes,
the reindeer awake
to Santa's call,
as he his gifts prepares:
as if to reflect the most precious gift
made to man,
two thousand years ago.

Joy Morton

CHRISTMAS

Snowflakes falling to form their mantle of white
everywhere is peaceful on this holy night.
Dawn awakens to herald in this special day
footprints in the snow to guide us on our way.

Church bells ringing out for all to hear
sending out their message, loud and clear.
Christmas time is a season to be jolly
doors adorned with wreaths of holly.

Mistletoe hanging for all to see
fairy lights twinkling on the Christmas tree.
Pine logs burning on an open fire
Old stories being told that never seem to tire.

This day of days with its fun and joys
excited children playing with their toys.
The atmosphere is alive with Yuletide carols
games being played with painted barrels.

But never forget the first Christmas of all
a baby boy born in a lonely cattle stall.
We celebrate Christmas in our own different way
so rejoice and give thanks on our Lord's birthday.

Raymond Thomas Edwards

MORE THAN A MILE APART

Hold out that olive branch
Let your family know
You care, for love is rare
Do not let family rifts
Pile up like snowbound drifts.
Open up your hope and heart
Let love lift, so rare a gift.

Do not sit alone in gloom
Let the love inside you bloom
Send that Christmas card
Pick up the phone
Let your family know
You are coming home.

Let that love show through
Those lonely, darkened days
Do not be near-sighted
Wrongs can be righted
Forgiveness and joy
Was born with that little boy
So long ago, born to die.

Born to show the way
Just like the star on Christmas Day
Forgiveness binds families together
Knowing unconditional love
And the message is plain
God is love. He forgives
And you will live again.

Anne Marshall

MY CHRISTMAS WANTS

What do I want for Christmas? Many things that cash can't buy.
Firstly, love and peace all around, so no one has need to cry.
I want to know an end to war, wherever in the world,
Man at peace, with everyone, every battle flag - tight furled.
I want to feel again at midnight, as I stand among my stock,
that Christ has come, again to Earth, is here to lead his flock.
I want to find the magic, once, well known to me,
of seeing children's faces, as they gather round the tree.
I want to think, 'friends absent', will sometime, 'drink a toast',
to me and mine, as I to them. That again I will sometime be their host.
I want the greatest gift of all, to witness the *nativity,*
knowing *He* was born, to save all sinners, such as me.

Brian Muchmore

CHRISTMAS

Christmas is that time of year,
when we welcome all those we hold dear,
with warmth and festive cheer,
a loving hug to say, 'It's good to have you here'.

Christmas is that time of year,
when excited children rush around,
their energy knows no bounds,
and parents wish they would calm down.

Christmas is that time of year,
when thoughts of those who have left us appear,
how we still wish they were here,
and in a quiet moment we may shed a tear.

Christmas is that time of year,
when everyone eats too much,
having turkey for days is a bit tough,
we long for fish and chips, the simple stuff.

Christmas is that time of year,
when we think of others less fortunate than ourselves,
realising we are lucky to have enough food to eat,
and a comfortable place in which to sleep.

Julie Marie Laura Shearing

CHRISTMAS

Christmas is the season of goodwill for all;
for all those who believe
or who can afford.

Christmas, the season which highlights
difference and diversity:

the devout go to church
as they did the previous Sunday,
others find themselves
inside a church for the first time
since last year's carol service;

evangelical outreach groups
invite radio listeners to text in
for the true Christmas message
and Christian-based charities
advertise their Christmas appeals;

bright neon-lit night-clubs
host themed Christmas parties,
backstreet smoke-filled pubs
smell of beer and old men's burps;

TV adverts are filled with CDs, DVDs,
toys and perfumes,
soon to be replaced by sun-filled holidays.

The true meaning of Christmas
is different for us all:

eating, drinking, living to excess;
a time for religious contemplation;
or just another day of surviving.

Matt Ebeling

CHRISTMAS

Christmas is *supposed* to be a happy time for families to share
All the nice and lovely things that are waiting there
There are carols sung in every store till by Christmas - do we
want more?
But it gives such a happy feeling as our tired senses all start reeling.

Have I got the Christmas pud, and that scarf for Jane?
Last year I *know* I bought her something else, it wouldn't do to buy
the same
And now for Christmas Day itself, get all the gifts down from the shelf
I wish we didn't have to ask Father, he just sits now - so perhaps he'd
rather stay again in the folk's home, he's safe in there for he can't roam.

But now - that's not the Christmas spirit, families should all be together
Where hearts are bonded to each other and travel out whate'er the
weather
Have I made time to go to church and see the Christ child there
And listen quietly to the carols and sit awhile in prayer?

Or have I left too little time amidst the turkey and the wine
to set aside a prayer for Him, will He hear above the din?
O what a tinsel world we live in now, as bare as leaves upon the bough
Somehow, somewhere, we're missing out, on what Christmas
really is all about.

When last did you call your friend, you *know* she's suffering no end
For her Christmas will bring no respite, for her nothing will ever be
- quite right
When did you last call someone you love, never mind *what* they're
guilty of
All right so what they did hurt you, forgive, forget and start anew.

When did you last hug your little girl instead of being in such a whirl
And stop to sing and dance with her, never mind being in such a tear
Your husband too, he needs you, he's done his best this year
He's worked and struggled in this recession, could *you* not make
the same concession?

And what about your little boy, don't fob him off with some new toy
For all our families need is love, so let's give thanks to God above
And celebrate this Christmas time, with our dear Lord's bread
and wine!

Janet Robertson Jones

WHY?

Why were we born
Why are we here?
Time rolls by
Before the reason is clear.

Jesus was born
As the Bible foretold,
Wise Men visited him with
Frankincense, myrrh and gold.

Shepherds in a field
Followed a shining star,
His birth is celebrated
By all, near and far.

Goodwill to all men
He came to say,
Love one another,
Thank God for each day.

Why do men not heed
This message of goodwill?
We all pray for peace.
Not wars that kill!

Stella Bush-Payne

THE VOICE OF CHRISTMAS

Where trees have echoed long in winter's flow'r,
And snow has laid so evenly around,
In branches singing gladly robin's hour,
Her sweet and mellow silence to surround;
That holly choirs upon the gentle tune,
Among the hanging berries, rich in frost,
Where angels play once more and favour soon,
In wand'ring eyes, awoken from the lost;
Where gifts delight again the smiling tree,
And wrap around the child of Christmas joy,
So watching o'er unfolding dreams will see,
In loving eyes, in ev'ry girl and boy;
Each child was born this Christmas night again,
Draws near and near, a child we still remain.

Christopher W Wolfe

SANTA

When Santa wakes up from his sleep
He fills his sack with toys
And wonders if he has enough
For all the girls and boys?

He sets off to feed his reindeer
And makes sure they're all well fed
He checks the most important thing
To see Rudolf's nose is red.

He piles the toys upon the sleigh
And packs them in quite tight
He doesn't want to lose them
When the reindeer are in flight.

Now that everything is ready
Into the sleigh he goes
He pulls the reins and off they go
Helped out by Rudolf's nose.

The sky's so dark 'part from the stars
There's nothing else in sight
For Santa is the only one
Who works so late at night.

He delivers all his presents
And eats up all his treats
He gives a friendly, 'Ho, ho, ho!'
To anyone he meets.

With his sleigh completely empty
Santa knows the job's done well
But will everyone be happy
Only hours and he can tell.

Before he settles down to bed
Santa checks out what he's done
He looks down upon the families
And children having fun.

Happy with all that he sees
Santa pulls his night-cap on
He settles beneath the covers
And falls asleep with a yawn.

J L Preston

WHEN CHRIST WAS BORN ON CHRISTMAS DAY

When Christ was born on Christmas Day
A manger was His bed
The night was dark, the inns were full
So He slept in a shed.
And on a hill not far away
The angels sang a song
The shepherds heard and were afraid
To see the holy throng.

The shepherds came to see the child
As He lay in the straw
They bowed down and they worshipped Him
Humbly upon the floor
And wise men from a distant land
Beheld a holy star
They followed 'til they found the child
They travelled from afar.

The wise men, they brought gifts to Him
The newborn king of kings
Gold, frankincense and myrrh they brought
A gift of royal things.
Now up in Heaven above us
The party's underway
They know the victory's in sight
And we'll be there some day.

Sharon Elton

INFORMATION

We hope you have enjoyed reading this book - and that you will continue to enjoy it in the coming years.

If you like reading and writing poetry drop us a line, or give us a call, and we'll send you a free information pack.

Alternatively if you would like to order further copies of this book or any of our other titles, then please give us a call or log onto our website at www.forwardpress.co.uk

Anchor Books Information
Remus House
Coltsfoot Drive
Peterborough
PE2 9JX
(01733) 898102